Offset or uncoated paper has a very rough finish. Unlike coated paper, with its glossy appearance and ability to have a textured coating applied on it, this material is porous and absorbs ink.

BOOKS
AND THE
PEOPLE WHO
MAKE THEM

The body text determines the size of the font. In this book, the characters are written in size **9pt**.

This paper has a gram weight of **170 gr.** This relates to the weight of the paper in grams per square meter. The lower the weight, the finer and more flexible the paper.

PRESTEL

MUNICH · LONDON · NEW YORK

The author — p. 4

The editor — p. 8

The illustrator — p. 12

The graphic designer — p. 16

The sales representative — p. 20

The printer — p. 24

The bookseller — p. 28

The literary critic — p. 32

The librarian — p. 36

The readers — p. 40

Dear Readers,

I don't know where or how you discovered this book—perhaps it was a gift? Maybe you came across it on a table at a bookstore? Or you may have borrowed it from your local library. Well, no matter how it happened, I am glad this book made it into your hands. That's because a book without a reader is like a turtle without a shell. It makes no sense! To be honest with you, I had originally planned to focus this book on a completely different subject, but my editor convinced me to take an interest in what goes on behind the scenes in the world of publishing. I then realized that creating a book is first and foremost about one thing, and that is teamwork! So prepare to learn about a heap of things to do with BOOKS and the people that make them.

For you, dear readers, I conducted a thorough investigation into this subject. I sneaked into an illustrator's studio, a bookstore, and a library; rubbed shoulders with graphic designers and printers; and even managed to slip into some very confidential meetings—all so I could reveal to you the secrets of these exceptional professions! Welcome to the world of books!

The Author

The Author

The author is without a doubt the true starting point of a book.

When we talk about authors, we immediately think about the writers of great novels. There are, however, a great many types of books in the world—novels form just a small part of the range of works that exist. No matter how different they are on the inside, however, all books have certain things in common. A graphic novel, school textbook, and tourist guide, for example, all consist of bound pages and carry that distinct ink-and-paper smell.

No matter the book, the author is always the one who writes it. The author brings us into their world by inventing stories or communicating knowledge. Reading is all about seeing the world through the eyes of the writer.

Ode to Turtles

TURTLES FOR DUMMIES

ENCYCLO-
PEDIA OF
TURTLES

BIG GUIDE TO TURTLES

IN SEARCH OF THE GIANT TURTLE OF GALÁPAGOS

How is the idea for a book born?

The idea for a book may be the outcome of many years of labor, or it may arrive suddenly by chance. The English novelist Mary Shelley created Frankenstein's monster in the wake of a dream in which the creature appeared to her. Harry Potter began to take shape in JK Rowling's mind during a train journey from London to Manchester.

The manuscripts of great authors say a lot about the way they work. Those of Marcel Proust contain text that is crossed out and underlined, and some paragraphs have even been rewritten in the margins. When the passages he wanted to add were too long, he copied them onto little bits of paper and glued them to his notebook.

My Big Encyclopedia of Turtles

Turtles: EVERYTHING You Need to Know

Searching for Turtles

TURTLES

The name we read on the cover of a book is not always the name of the person who wrote it! To protect their private lives or those around them, some writers publish under an alias. The Portuguese author Fernando Pessoa was a master of this, as were others including Aurore Dupin (alias George Sand) and Charlotte Brontë (alias Currer Bell). In fact, many female authors have chosen male pen names to help their books be published and recognized.

Sometimes manuscripts can disappear.
It is December 1996, and the French novelist Georges Perec is in the process of moving to a new home. He burrows about, throwing old papers into one case and his latest efforts into another. He intends to keep hold of the manuscripts and throw away the old papers...but he does the opposite! This is how Perec lost one of his first works, *Portrait of a Man Known as Il Condottiere*, which was rediscovered in 1982, 10 years after his death, and finally published in 2012.

Some of the great masterpieces of the 20th century were written on the typewriter.
This machine popularized the QWERTY keyboard that we know today. Why this name? The letters were placed so that the most frequently used ones were spaced out. This prevented the printing hammers of the typewriter from getting jammed.

A book is a collective venture, and writing is not always the first stage...

The original idea for a book may stem from the editor, who then commissions the writer. An illustrated project could start with the artist before the author has even written the text.

Nowadays, the first draft of a book is often typed using the keyboard of a computer. The keyboard may be very different depending on where the author comes from. For example, the Spanish keyboard includes a second letter 'n' with the *tilde* inflection (ñ) as well as the inverted exclamation point (¡). Like English-language keyboards, the Japanese keyboard is all about phonetics, meaning it allows the user to input letters (known as *kana*) representing various sounds. A software may then translate the words into kanji (Chinese characters).

A pop-up book can sometimes be proposed by the paper specialist, who has designed the model of the book before the writer has even thought of it.

How is the author paid?
The author usually receives a percentage of the book's price. For example, if each book is sold at fifteen dollars, the author may earn royalties of 7%, or one dollar and fifty cents for each book sold. The author's slice of the cake is, therefore, not a very large one! The rest will go for printing, distribution, and to all the other players along the so-called book chain. The publisher generally pays an advance to the author, who keeps that sum regardless of the number of copies sold. Out of all the authors in the world, the number who can live off the strength of their pen is low.

Writing is often a solitary activity, but that need not always be the case. The Russian author, Dostoyevsky, for example, dictated his novels directly to a stenographer, who typed the text on a typewriter.

In France, Boris Vian used to run his book concepts by his wife, Michelle Léglise, who then contributed ideas and suggested edits to the author. She played a big role in the creation of his novels.

Hello and thank you very much for your manuscript. Turtles are unfortunately not a very popular subject, and we only just published your previous work on this same subject last year. Perhaps you could think about writing a book devoted to another of your passions, such as...

OCTOBER

TO DO

The Editor

A great number of manuscripts are sent to publishing houses every day, each with the hope of getting published. Just a small number of these will eventually find a place in a bookstore! Before going ahead with a title, an editor has a huge amount to consider. They need to be intuitive and knowledgeable about the book market and only keep hold of those projects they truly believe in. The editor's role is also to unearth new talents: authors and illustrators.

Even after a manuscript is accepted, it cannot be published just as it was received. Sometimes, a text must be reworked with the writer, translated, if it was written in a foreign language, possibly illustrated, and then copy edited. Next come the issues of layout, choices of format and the kind of paper to use, followed by a final proofread. The editor, therefore, works in tandem with several professionals right up to the point when the book can be presented to the commercial team focused on selling it to bookstores.

According to the British Publishers Association, the UK is the largest exporter of books in the world. There are over 200 publishers in the UK and Ireland, and around 300 in the USA and Canada. Some publishers can only produce small volumes of books annually, whilst others are huge editorial groups that put out thousands of titles each year.

Whether it is to do with style, plot, or the flow of the narrative, a text can be extensively reworked following exchanges between the author and editor, who takes on the role of literary advisor. Gordon Lish, editor of the American writer Raymond Carver, pushed this practice very far. Much against his author's will, he drastically trimmed his texts to the point where they took on a dry, raw, and minimalist style…which led to Carver becoming immensely famous!

We talk a lot about the editor, but there are thousands of other professions in a publishing house. These include editorial assistants, artistic directors, graphic designers, specialist technical print makers, publishing directors, proofreaders, book publicity and marketing managers, foreign translation rights managers, translators, accountants… Each role plays a part in ensuring that the book is successful.

POSITIVE
A-
TTI-
TUDE

Flat plan
Books and the People
Who Make Them—Draft

→ CALL GRAPHIC DESIGNER! URGENT!

Appt
with
dentist
Tuesday,
1:30pm

Request
paper sample

This little grid is called the flat plan. It is an important step between the manuscript and the printed text, which shows where text and illustrations will be placed inside the book. This helps the editorial team to anticipate the number of pages needed, and reflects how the book is coming along.

14 15 16 17 18 19

24 25 26 27 28 29

Print run test

→ CHOOSE
TITLE
BEFORE
MONDAY

When a book is to be published abroad, the editor appoints a translator, whose job is to interpret the text in the spirit of the original. This is imaginative work! The translated text is also protected by copyright, like the original. Several translations of the same book, each bearing a unique title, can follow. The French 19th century novelist Alexandre Dumas's novel *The Count of Monte Christo* was not always known by that title. The first single-volume translation in English was entitled *The Prisoner of If or the Revenge of Monte Christo*.

Lunch with Antoine on 22nd

Every book gets its own choice of paper. Together with the graphic designer, the editor must select the paper for the inside of the book, the sleeve, and the covers. Among the deciding factors are the quality, the "feel" (page and book thickness), and the price. However, it is not always easy to predict the final outcome. So, the editor sometimes requests a mock-up that allows the editor to see what the final book will look like. Finally, the paper is purchased from a specialist paper maker or supplied through the printer. The quality of the paper and the number of copies to be printed will have a major impact on the budget for the book and therefore on its selling price.

When the book is designed, the editor receives the first layout. The editor may share this with the author. Together, they need to check that everything is in line with the very latest corrections. This last stage is called the final proof and upon signing off on this, the author and editor are giving the go-ahead to print.

The Illustrator

The illustrator tells their own version of the story in pictures and is as much the author of the book as the person writing the text. There are so many types of illustrated works, ranging from comic strips to children's books, documentary books, art books, and more. Sometimes, text and artwork are created by the same person. Other times, the images may have been created before the text, or both may have been conceived at the same time but by two separate people. There are also many illustrated books with no text whatsoever. Inside some books, illustrations may appear as a complete page, in others as motifs that punctuate the text. In short, all combinations are possible!

Turtle: Reptile

Tomi Ungerer, author of *The Three Robbers* and *Zeralda's Ogre*, spent many childhood hours copying countless illustrations from encyclopedias. He wanted to learn how to draw everything to the last detail. When he was asked as an adult what book he would take to a desert island he replied—the French Larousse Encyclopedia.

Antoine de Saint-Exupéry's watercolors contributed to making his book *The Little Prince* so hugely well known. In the gouache technique he used, several coats of paint are applied one after the other. The paint dries and is diluted once again upon coming in contact with the following application. The trick is knowing how to control the applications so that the previous layers of paint don't disappear—unlike normal watercolor paint, gouache paint is opaque.

The pencil is one of the most frequently used artists' tools and allows you to sketch ideas on paper in just a few strokes. Closely associated with childhood, the colored pencil remains a much-favored tool of the trade for many artists such as the Belgian illustrator Kitty Crowthe, who uses them to enhance her pastel drawings.

Engraving works according to the buffer principle, whereby a raised support (a type of matrix) is created, soaked in ink, and then pressed down on paper. From the *Fables of Fontaine* to the tales of Charles Perrault, Gustave Doré remains the master in this field!

Like many illustrators, Hergé, the creator of *Tintin*, conceived numerous pencil sketches before he finalized his comic strips. He erased and started afresh until he finally got the perfect line. He then copied his drawings onto tracing paper to achieve a perfect work with well-defined contours. This style of working is called ligne claire. Hergé then handed the work over to his teammates, the colorists, who created the final piece in color.

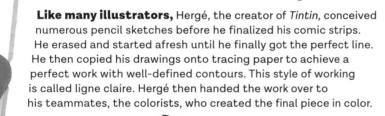

The editor

Certain illustrators mix and match techniques. Design, painting, and collage work can be superimposed on the computer to come up with an original image. Today, many illustrators work exclusively on the computer.

"What is the use of a book without pictures or conversations?" thinks Alice at the beginning of her adventures in *Alice in Wonderland.* Her words were taken seriously! Lewis Carroll's masterpiece was first illustrated by John Tenniel. Many others have also put their own spin on illustrating the text, such as the Spanish painter Salvador Dalí, the avant-garde artist Yayoi Kusama, and the illustrators Anthony Browne and Rébecca Dautremer. Thanks in part to such illustrations, Alice became one of the most popular figures in literature!

Some characters from children's books enjoy international success. When the Finnish artist Tove Jansson created the *Moomins* in 1945, she had no idea that her little round trolls would captivate the whole planet. They've since shown up as games, clothes, animated characters and even on the hull of an airplane! To this day, the Swedish illustrator Cecilia Heikkilä continues to bring their universe to life.

Storytelling can sometimes be achieved without writing. The illustration creates the story on its own. Visionary artists like Bruno Munari from Italy and Katsumi Komagata from Japan have made this their specialty. By playing with shapes, colors, and cutouts, they aim to surprise readers and invite them to touch and feel the book as an object. Initially sensory, reading allows plenty of room for the imagination.

The graphic designer

The graphic designer lays out the book. They select the fonts for the text, its size, and the line placing. Everything plays an important role to ensure reading is pleasurable. The graphic designer brings a rhythm and personality to the whole layout. With input from the editor, the graphic designer creates the cover of the book and chooses the finishes. The cover has to be memorable; after all, it's what tells us what we are going to read.

The images, color, and typography of the book must catch the reader's eye at the bookstore. Sometimes, we notice the novels of a particular publisher over thousands of others, thanks to the talent of the graphic designer. Following the correction and proofing stage, the graphic designer will input any necessary changes and prepare the pages so they are finally ready for print.

HATE COMIC SANS

AGENDA

What is the type area?
This is the space on the printed page occupied by blocks of text, and includes the surrounding margins or "gutter." It is framed by the bleed area, which gets trimmed off after printing.

There is a wide range of letter shapes and ways of putting letters beside each other. This is what typography is all about. Done well, it assists reading, creates a pleasant visual experience, and embellishes the pages. The shape of the letters changes the meaning of what we read. For example, the effect of **BIG, BLACK, CAPITAL LETTERS** versus thin, lower-case lettering is completely different!

The white on the page also plays a major role. It surrounds the strap lines, sets the paragraphs apart, isolates the stanzas in a poem, fills the margins, and frames the text. The white alone can create the elegance of a layout.

Fonts are often named after their creators. Claude Garamond, for example, gave his name to the famous typeface we still use today.

The page to the left is always an even number, at least in those languages that read from left to right. In Hebrew, Arabic, and in the Japanese manga style, odd and even pages are the other way around!

The first ever punctuation mark was the white space between words. Itwouldbeverydifficultforusnowadaystodecipheratext if the words were not separated. This *scriptio continua* or writing-without-spaces-style was still practiced until the 12th century in England. The use of dots, however, helped texts to be read more easily.

The drop cap is a large letter, often decorative, that is placed at the very beginning of a text. It was used in manuscripts in the Middle Ages, especially by monks who would be copying down religious texts. Nowadays, we still use drop caps sometimes, for example for the beginning letter of a new chapter.

With feathered banner texts, the lines are aligned to either the left or the right. A good feathered text avoids chopping words and aims to set all the lines to different lengths.

On the other hand, every line is the same length with block texts! The choice of how a text is aligned dictates its shape.

Bold type is generally used to emphasize a word, in contrast to Roman characters, which are much thinner.

Italics, letters that lean toward the right, owe their name to their place of birth. Among other things, they are used to highlight words written in a foreign language.

The page to the right is the one you first see when you open a book on the right-hand side. They always have an odd number. This is where the graphic designer most often positions anything they wish to highlight, such as illustrations or the start of a chapter.

The color chart is often used by graphic designers to choose the different shades they are going to use when typesetting. The chart allows colors to be seen as they are printed and not as they appear on the screen, which is sometimes very different.

2 3
4 5
6 7
8 9
10 11
12 13
14 15
16 17
18 19
20 21

Colors
C ———— 0%
M ———— 50%
Y ———— 100%
K ———— 0%

Meeting with sales rep at 10:30 am, April 30th

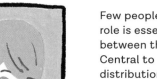

The sales representative

Few people know what the representative does, yet this role is essential. The sales representative is the link between the publishing house and the bookstore. Central to the commercial team known as sales and distribution, they call on bookstores to show them what titles are in the pipeline with the editor and to attract orders or, in other words, make sales. This person helps sell titles that they may not even have read themselves (but that has been extensively recommended by editors!). The representative is responsible for a particular geographical sector and is very familiar with the preferences of the bookstores in that sector. Their objective is to best advise bookstores according to their tastes and those of their customers. They can also gather feedback from the bookstores about the titles. The observations of the representative are invaluable and may even lead to last-minute changes in pricing, the cover, or even the title!

THE BIRDS OF SAN SEB.

What is a bestseller?
It is not so easy to determine when a book can be considered a bestseller. Newspapers and magazines like the New York Times or Publishers Weekly collect sales numbers from bookstores. Because they do not ask all the same booksellers and consider different time frames, their bestseller lists tend to differ. However, it is generally accepted that a book is a bestseller when it sells at least 5,000 copies per week.

What are the most popular books sold worldwide?
Without a doubt, the number one bestseller is the Bible, which holds a number of records. It is thought to be the first book ever printed and has been translated into 698 languages. The Hobbit and The Little Prince have each sold over 150 million copies globally. And the first volume of Harry Potter alone has sold 120 million copies!

While the sales team looks after the bookstores, the book is also presented by other teams to film producers for a possible TV or film adaptation and to foreign book editors in the hope of getting it translated into other languages... A large format book may have a second life in the form of comic strips, on a performance stage, at the movie theater, or on the radio!

A good representative must have a drivers' license and a taste for travel! He or she is frequently on the road visiting bookstores to present the new titles for publication. After catching up with the bookseller, the representative takes the order. Some small publishers take meetings with the booksellers themselves to market their books. This is called self-promotion!

CINEMA
10 PM
THE SHINING

In 1935, British publisher Allen Lane launched Penguin Books. Believing that good books should not cost more than a pack of cigarettes, he started selling reprints of successful books in paperback format. The books were only sixpence and color-coded: orange for fiction, blue for biography, and green for crime. Novels by Agatha Christie and Ernest Hemingway were among the first ten books Lane published.

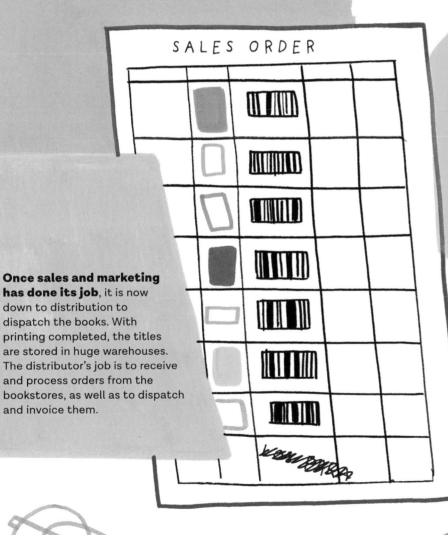

SALES ORDER

Once sales and marketing has done its job, it is now down to distribution to dispatch the books. With printing completed, the titles are stored in huge warehouses. The distributor's job is to receive and process orders from the bookstores, as well as to dispatch and invoice them.

= map.

The printer

The printer receives digital files from the publisher and uses them to make the book. Before printing, the printer runs tests to check how the colors look. If these are not satisfactory, they are corrected. Printing is carried out on two different types of machines, namely sheet-fed presses and rotary presses, which are faster because the paper comes from a roll.

The printing operation is performed in two phases: ink and color composition and then rolling. The first involves setting the printing plate until the quality of the first printed sheets is approved by the editor. Rolling refers to the mechanical printing of the paper until the desired number is reached.

Finally, the printed paper is shaped. The sheets are folded, sometimes sewn together with thread to be bound, and glued to the spine and cover.

The book is now ready to meet its readers.

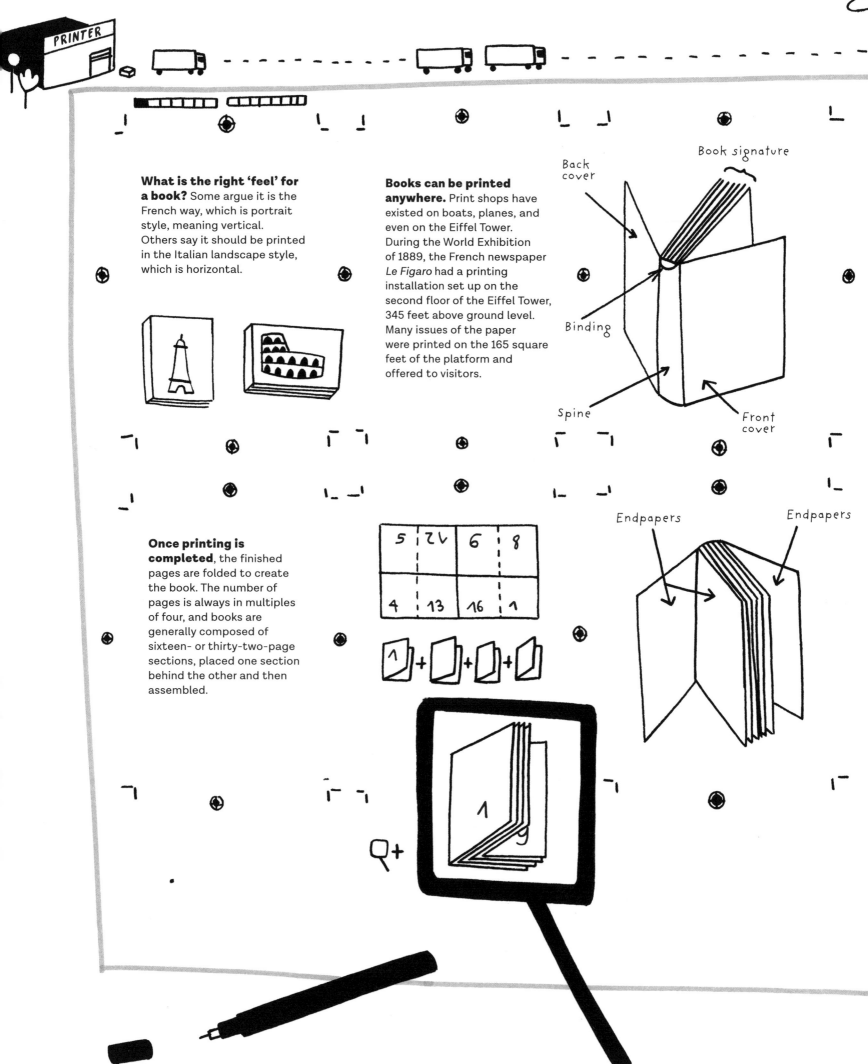

What is the right 'feel' for a book? Some argue it is the French way, which is portrait style, meaning vertical. Others say it should be printed in the Italian landscape style, which is horizontal.

Books can be printed anywhere. Print shops have existed on boats, planes, and even on the Eiffel Tower. During the World Exhibition of 1889, the French newspaper *Le Figaro* had a printing installation set up on the second floor of the Eiffel Tower, 345 feet above ground level. Many issues of the paper were printed on the 165 square feet of the platform and offered to visitors.

Back cover

Book signature

Binding

Spine

Front cover

Once printing is completed, the finished pages are folded to create the book. The number of pages is always in multiples of four, and books are generally composed of sixteen- or thirty-two-page sections, placed one section behind the other and then assembled.

Endpapers

Endpapers

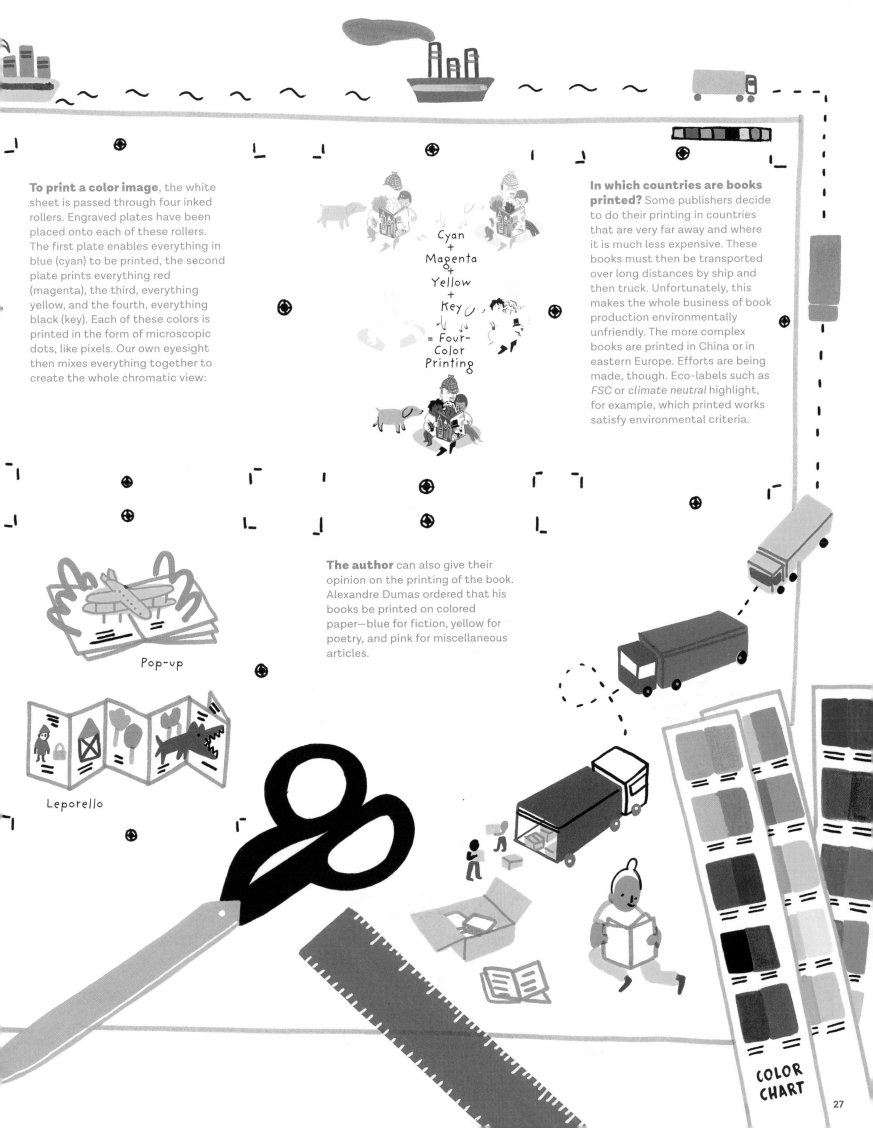

To print a color image, the white sheet is passed through four inked rollers. Engraved plates have been placed onto each of these rollers. The first plate enables everything in blue (cyan) to be printed, the second plate prints everything red (magenta), the third, everything yellow, and the fourth, everything black (key). Each of these colors is printed in the form of microscopic dots, like pixels. Our own eyesight then mixes everything together to create the whole chromatic view:

Cyan
+
Magenta
+
Yellow
+
Key
=
Four-
Color
Printing

In which countries are books printed? Some publishers decide to do their printing in countries that are very far away and where it is much less expensive. These books must then be transported over long distances by ship and then truck. Unfortunately, this makes the whole business of book production environmentally unfriendly. The more complex books are printed in China or in eastern Europe. Efforts are being made, though. Eco-labels such as *FSC* or *climate neutral* highlight, for example, which printed works satisfy environmental criteria.

Pop-up

Leporello

The author can also give their opinion on the printing of the book. Alexandre Dumas ordered that his books be printed on colored paper—blue for fiction, yellow for poetry, and pink for miscellaneous articles.

COLOR CHART

27

The bookseller

Forthcoming titles, the latest news, and book prices…the bookstore owner has to be aware of everything to enable him or her to support and advise readers. Far from just spending the days reading, a bookseller has lots to do: shelving books received, running stock checks, looking after the display cases, meeting sales reps from publishing houses, and even planning events, book signings, and kids' workshops. These are tasks vital to the life of a bookstore, which is first and foremost a business. Bookstores are all very different from each other, from small neighborhood shops to major industry players right through to very specialized stores.

NOVEL

CONFESSIONS

ALL YOU NEED TO KNOW ABOUT
TURTLES

Gaston

CHRISTIAN
ROBINSON ♡

New Release

Bookstores aim to order a certain number of new releases that are being marketed each season. Should they not sell, a bookseller can return them to the publisher provided none of the books have been damaged.

At checkout, the bookseller scans the barcode of the book. The numbers at the bottom of the barcode are the EAN (European Article Number). All the books in the world have one of these and they begin either with 978 or 979. The other digits specify the country of origin, then the publishing house, the catalogue number associated with this particular book, and finally, the check digit.

Books are my bag is the slogan of Bookshop Day celebrated in the UK and Ireland in October every year. The campaign wants to celebrate books and the people who sell them. Each year, famous children's book illustrators design a beautiful tote bag that can only be purchased in bookshops. In the US, independent bookstores are honored annually on the last Saturday of April. On that day, independent bookshops run events such as concerts or readings and sell special edition books or literary items that cannot be bought on any other day.

LONG
AWAITED

A bookstore like Libreria Acqua Alta could only exist in Venice. It has a view of the canals and is home to many cats. Over 100,000 books, occupying every corner of the store, can be found among this chaos. And you have to collect the books by boat, bathtub, or even a gondola! In Paris, the mythical English bookstore Shakespeare and Co invites artists and writers to sleep among the books. The number of visitors to have spent a night there is estimated to be over 30,000, and it is still possible to do this nowadays!

Sometimes, mistakes are discovered right at the moment of a book's publication! The erratum, coming from the Latin *errare* or 'to err' in English, is a little page placed within the book containing a list of corrections. Sometimes, the publisher asks the bookseller to insert this into the books that have already arrived.

And what happens to the books that are not sold? Booksellers are allowed to return the books they did not sell. Publishers may then try to sell them at a lower price. These books are called remainders. However, sometimes books get "pulped," meaning they are destroyed and the paper is recycled.

If you could see that

I'm the one

Who understands you

Been here all along

So why can't you see

You belong with me

Vol 1

Vol 2

Vol 3

Vol 4

Vol 5

Vol 6

In most parts of the world, booksellers can set their own prices. Major bookstores, which buy large quantities of stock from publishers, tend to get bigger discounts and can therefore offer books at lower prices than smaller bookshops. Some countries, like Germany or Italy for example, have fixed prices for books, so that all bookstores have to offer them at the same price. This is done to allow smaller shops to remain competitive with big retailers, and helps promote specialized bookstores like comic book or fantasy bookstores.

Staff Pick

signed copies

Of course, books are sold in more locations than bookstores alone. Other places include large chain stores or supermarkets, museums, cultural sites, and press agencies, to name just a few. Books are also sold more and more online, but the curated selection of the bookstore, the bookseller's advice, and their personal recommendations are not to be found on the internet. To support the creation of the book and its entire chain, it is important to buy books from bookstores.

The oldest bookstore in the world is in Lisbon, Portugal. La Livraria Bertrand was established in 1732 and is still open today!

ERRA-TUM

Persuasion

The literary critic

The literary critic works on the radio, on television, or in written media. Sometimes one person can work in all three! New books arrive at the editorial office of newspapers almost every day, often before publication. The critic must therefore read a lot and quickly form an opinion on titles that are about to appear. Then they have to give a thoughtful opinion on these texts, highlighting their qualities and shortcomings. Book critics are writers in their own field. They need to arouse the interest of the readers and dive deeply into the book they are writing about. Surprisingly, even bad reviews can be helpful, because just talking about a book gives it a better chance of not being forgotten.

NOTES

Alas...another book about books. Couldn't the author just stick to what he knows? We would have appreciated a knowledgeable summary of all the different species of underwater turtles. Instead, we get a chatty book on a subject that is well known to bookstores, libraries and readers alike—the book!

CULTURE
Press

PLEASE SEE MY PRESS OFFICER

The literary critic works closely with the media services of publishing houses to stay informed about new releases, meet up with authors during the book's promotion period, and so on. The critic's contact is the press officer, who hands out the press and media packs, organizes promotional tours and events for writers, and spends a lot of time on the phone with journalists, bloggers, and the authors too!

BEFORE PUBLICATION, THE AUTHOR WILL OFTEN SIGN a certain number of books that will be sold at bookstores or given away to fans. Historically, the signing or dedication was a tribute from the author to those who had given them money to live off their pen—maybe a prince or their patron.

WHAT IS THE SCHEDULE?

The publisher never chooses the publication date of the book by accident. Christmas time is the best release period for fine or high-quality books, children's books, and books marketed as gifts. At the end of August, the press starts to focus on new releases, because fall is the season of literary awards and the Frankfurt Book Fair, the world's largest trade fair for books.

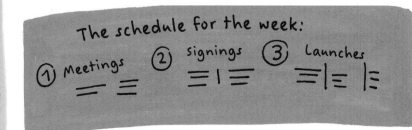

"Hercule Poirot Is Dead"

When Agatha Christie decided that Hercule Poirot was to make his exit, the death of the Belgian detective upset the whole world. On August 6, 1975, the *New York Times* published an obituary titled: "Hercule Poirot Is Dead." This was the first time that a daily newspaper devoted an obituary to a character from a novel.

Prize-worthy

The Booker Prize for the best novel written in English, the Women's Prize for Fiction, the Hugo Award for the best Science Fiction writers and the PEN America Literary Awards—there are many awards honoring writers of different genres. The Hans Christian Andersen Award is considered the highest recognition given to authors and illustrators of children's books. Other awards for children's literature are the Klaus Flugge Prize, the John Newbury Medal and the Golden Kite Awards. These prestigious awards are generally advertised by a sticker placed on the book.

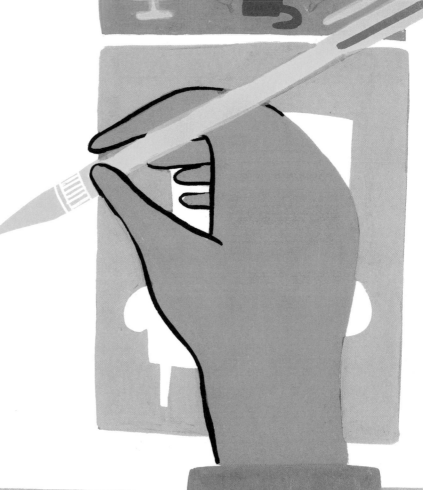

Children's literature

BOOKS
AND THE PEOPLE WHO MAKE THEM

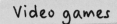
Video games

The librarian

The librarian, like the bookseller, is a link between the book and the reader. They welcome the public, classify the books, and arrange their lending. Most of the work, however, takes place in an office and far away from the bookshelves! Often responsible for a section, the librarian prepares and protects the books, and also enriches the library's stock…With advice from bookstores, they decide on the selection of books as well as magazines, DVDs, and sheet music. The librarian takes on board readers' feedback and, of course, must remain within the available budget. Libraries are precious places. You can visit them free of charge, meet authors, attend exhibitions, listen to live talks or readings, and then go on your way with a bagful of new discoveries!

YA

LIBRARY

The Christmas selection

Computers

Wifi

DVDs

Fine Arts

Exhibitions

Reading corner

Fiction

Non-Fiction

There are around 3,000 public libraries in the UK and around 9,000 in the USA. The Library of Congress in Washington D.C., USA, is the biggest in the world. It contains more than 173 million items. With around 170 million items, the British Library in London in is slightly smaller. Still, it would take more than 80,000 years to peruse the whole collection if one looked at five books every day.

When it comes to accessing culture, libraries have a huge role to play throughout the world. In the Nkayi district in Zimbabwe, mobile libraries pulled by donkeys travel out to visit remote communities. These have been hugely successful. A major part of the population in this region has learned how to read thanks to these mobile libraries.

How can we inspire young people to visit libraries? Exhibitions, themed screenings, video game sections, reading clubs…Many libraries have come up with ideas devoted to bringing in more users, whether they come for books or not. In Oslo, Norway, at the famous Biblo Tøyen, young children and adults are excluded. This library is purely reserved for 10–15 year olds! It is fitted out with old vehicles, pickup trucks transformed into a kitchen bar, mechanical lift cabins… The teenagers organize the books according to subject matter by themselves, mixing fiction and non-fiction.

Libraries maintain a permanent collection, and then there are certain books that join in and some that leave! Every year a kind of weeding out occurs, meaning that damaged or outdated books are removed to make room on the shelves for new ones. These are usually given away to readers or sold at a very low price.

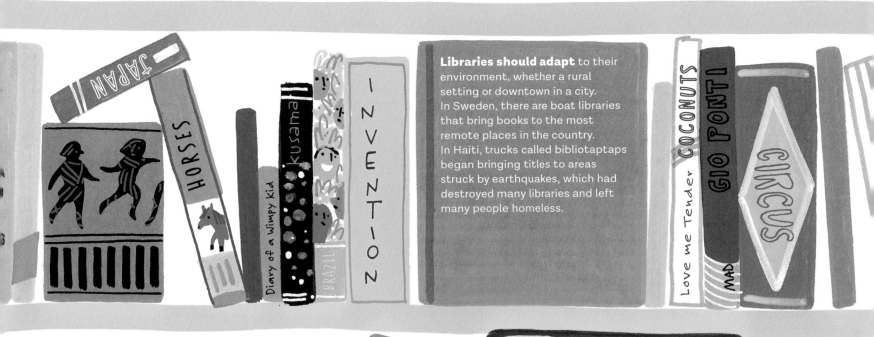

Libraries should adapt to their environment, whether a rural setting or downtown in a city. In Sweden, there are boat libraries that bring books to the most remote places in the country. In Haiti, trucks called bibliotaptaps began bringing titles to areas struck by earthquakes, which had destroyed many libraries and left many people homeless.

Libraries can be found in a variety of places, such as day cares, schools, hospitals, and prisons! Provided you don't suffer motion sickness, it is even possible to read in taxis in Brazil. In São Paulo, passengers using the Bibliotaxi service can borrow books placed in pouches behind the driver's seat, take them home and later return them in another taxi that is part of the scheme.

Although they are still quite rare, digital libraries are starting to appear. BiblioTech in San Antonio, Texas, is the first all-digital library in the United States, where you will find electronic devices in the place of books. Fully digitized libraries have been project tested in airports, like those in Philadelphia in the USA or in Amsterdam in the Netherlands.

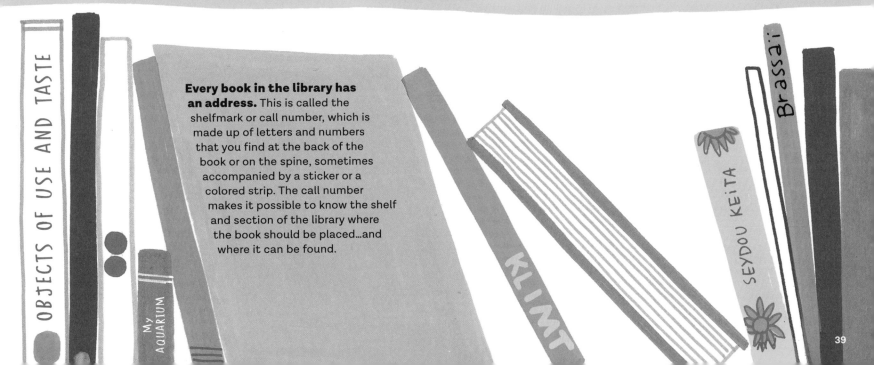

Every book in the library has an address. This is called the shelfmark or call number, which is made up of letters and numbers that you find at the back of the book or on the spine, sometimes accompanied by a sticker or a colored strip. The call number makes it possible to know the shelf and section of the library where the book should be placed…and where it can be found.

It's spring!

The readers

Young or old, student or office worker, parent or child—there are as many types of readers in the world as there are books. Moreover, there are just as many ways of reading. At any age and whether you are sitting, lying down, on your stomach or on your back, reading is also a physical activity. Grab a book, lift it, open it, and close it again. This is baby gymnastics! Toddlers are already engaging in a form of reading just by grabbing the object. They touch it, turn the pages, eat it up visually, and sometimes even listen to it, in the case of the audio book or a book read aloud. Whether we know how to read or not, storytelling is only one part of reading anyway. For some, loving a book can mean simply scribbling in it! For others, it is all about taking extreme care of a book and treating it as if it were brand new. And some of us read to travel without leaving our armchairs, to meet new characters, real or imaginary, and to experience new adventures… Long live books!

A book can change the course of a reader's life or even change the law! *The Jungle,* written by Upton Sinclair and published in the United States in 1906, tells the story of a Lithuanian immigrant who moves with his family to Chicago from the slaughterhouse district of New York. The description of the meat business caused a scandal in the US at the time and prompted President Theodore Roosevelt to change the law in this business.

Sometimes, it is the reader who changes the life of the author. The comic strip writer Riad Sattouf says he stopped smoking after a meeting at a book signing with one of his readers who was a lung specialist. And when a medical examiner pointed out to Pierre Lemaitre, the detective novelist, that he had made mistakes in many of the crime scenes in his works, she became a special advisor on his subsequent books!

When it gets too difficult to leave a literary universe, why not do it yourself? Fan fiction is a term for stories written and distributed by regular readers on the internet. These fans may choose to prolong the adventures of their heroes, or write a new version of events...Certain writers encourage this practice, whilst others, like George R.R. Martin, the author of *A Game of Thrones*, are staunchly against it!

If only characters on paper could exist in the real world...Indeed, some have chosen to make that possible. For about a century, some readers have imagined that the adventures of Sherlock Holmes really happened. They reconstruct what the character's "real" life would be from the novels of Arthur Conan Doyle. These Holmesologists also try to find explanations for the contradictions that occur in the detective's adventures. So, for example: "Why does Dr. Watson's wife call him James on an adventure, when his first name is actually John?"

How do you find a book in the library? Well, you have to look at the spine, the only visible part when the book is shelved. In English-speaking countries, you need to tilt your head toward the right when you read it. But in Germany or France, for example, it is the other way around.

Reading doesn't only make you smarter, it also makes you kinder. A study at the Kingston University in London has shown that people who read a lot are more empathetic and tend to be able to see things from other people's perspectives.

Surprisingly, the books that are most sought after by collectors are often those containing errors. These editions have never been reprinted identically, since they contain misprints. They are very rare and therefore very desirable!

The reader who owns the most expensive book in the world is the businessman Bill Gates. This is the Leicester Codex, which is a manuscript from the year 1500 containing 72 pages of specular writing by Leonardo da Vinci. Specular writing is reverse or mirror writing, which means you need a mirror to read it. Bill Gates bought the manuscript in 1994 for 30 million dollars. Today, that would be about 60 million dollars.

We do not always read with our eyes. A book can be listened to (thanks to audio-books) or read via touch if we are blind. The braille alphabet was invented by Louis Braille in 1829 and makes use of small, raised dots to convey meaning. Some works combine print and digital media, where the reading experience is extended on screen via animation, music, and even augmented reality.

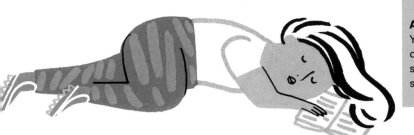

A book can have a thousand lives! Public book banks flourish everywhere. You can drop off books you have read at these places so that they can be discovered and passed around by other readers. These book recycling stations can be found in streets, parks, and sometimes strange locations such as former telephone booths and even inside old fridges!

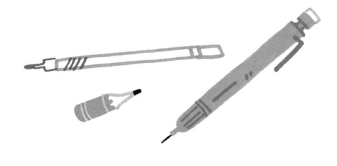

© for the French edition: 2022, Editions Arola.
All rights reserved.
Title of the original edition: *La grande aventure du livre*
This edition was published by arrangement with The Picture Book Agency, France.
© for the English edition: 2023, Prestel Verlag, Munich · London · New York
A member of Penguin Random House Verlagsgruppe GmbH
Neumarkter Strasse 28 · 81673 Munich
text: Stéphanie Vernet, 2022
illustrations: Camille de Cussac, 2022

Library of Congress Control Number: 2023932470
A CIP catalogue record for this book is available from the British Library.

Translated from the French by Paul Kelly

Project management: Constanze Holler, Fatima Grieser
Copy editing: Ayesha Wadhawan
Production management and typesetting: Susanne Hermann
Printing and binding: L.E.G.O., Vicenza

Our production is
climate neutral
ClimatePartner.com/14044-1912-1001
Print product

Prestel Publishing compensates the CO_2 emissions produced from the making of this book by supporting a reforestation project in Brazil.
Find further information on the project here:
www.ClimatePartner.com/14044-1912-1001

MIX
Paper | Supporting responsible forestry
FSC
www.fsc.org
FSC® C023419

Penguin Random House Verlagsgruppe
FSC® N001967

Printed in Italy
ISBN 978-3-7913-7549-6
www.prestel.com